ART AND CRAFTS
GLASS AND POTTERY

ARTS AND CRAFTS
GLASS AND POTTERY

Grange BOOKS

A QUANTUM BOOK

Published by Grange Books
an imprint of Grange Books Plc
The Grange
Kingsnorth Industrial Estate
Hoo, nr. Rochester
Kent ME3 9ND

1-84013-264-7

This book is produced by
Quantum Books Ltd
6 Blundell Street
London N7 9BH

Project Manager: Rebecca Kingsley
Project Editor: Judith Millidge
Designer: Wayne Humphries
Editor: Clare Haworth-Maden

The material in this publication previously appeared in
*The Arts and Crafts Movement, Introduction to the
Decorative Arts*

QUMACGP
Set in Times
Reproduced in Singapore by Eray Scan (Pte) Ltd
Printed in Singapore by Star Standard Industries (Pte) Ltd

CONTENTS

INTRODUCTION

Reactionary, revolutionary, romantic and rationalist are epithets applicable to the work of the men and women of the Arts and Crafts Movement on both sides of the Atlantic. A survey of the Arts and Crafts Movement, from its origins in the writings of Pugin, Carlyle and Ruskin to its effective demise in Nazi Germany, shows that it was nothing if not diverse. If the Arts and Crafts Movement is so varied a conglomeration of both theory and practice, what, then, binds it together as a movement?

Opposite: A design for a dado by the British artist Walter Crane.

Below: A potrait of William Morris, a cornerstone of the British Arts and Crafts Movement.

In order to appreciate the factors that bind Ruskin, Wright, Hubbard, Gropius, Morris and others together and to grasp the long-term significance of the Arts and Crafts Movement, one has first to take into account the aims and intentions of other movements in art over the past century or so.

Around the middle of the nineteenth century, an attitude evolved which maintained that art existed in a vacuum with no direct reference to the society from which it sprang. Art had no particular social use and those that produced it shunned public approval and, in some instances, deliberately courted public censure. This tendency was evident in the art and literature of nineteenth-century France. It was also apparent in the works of Wilde, Swinburne and Whistler, as well as in the aspirations of Art Nouveau, and it continued in a variety of forms throughout the twentieth century. The tradition continues in our own time, in that perfectly ordinary, intelligent people are quite unable to understand the art produced by their own society.

SOCIAL UTILITY

The notion that art is a highly refined activity with no particular role; that it has its own arcane, internal logic outside the grasp of the ordinary citizen; and that it is practised by

Right: The front page of the first edition of The Craftsman, *published by Stickley's United Crafts in the USA in 1904.*

specialists for specialists was vehemently rejected by many within the Arts and Crafts Movement. The movement, albeit in a number of ways, sought to afford art social utility. Under the protection of Pugin, art's purpose was to revive the architectural idiom of the Middle Ages and with it the finer spiritual feelings of the period. For Morris, art was predicated upon fulfiling work – and fulfiling work ultimately demanded vast social and economic change. In addition, art could be purged of much of its sophistication and refinement. For Morris and Ruskin, art became the democratic cultural expression of a community and needed no high priests in the form of artists to exercise the rite.

In the United States, the Arts and Crafts tradition was an aide to establishing a national identity founded upon independence, work and democracy. In Germany, the Arts and Crafts ideal again had a social application, be it (in Muthesius' case) to fashion a cultural and economic identity for bourgeois Germany or (in the case of the Bauhaus), to propagate, with the aid of machinery, logically designed, mass-produced goods for mass markets.

Public utility and a missionary zeal to improve the lots of producer and consumer are the only call to which all craftsmen and -women associated with the Arts and Crafts Movement could easily rally. The call was, however, quite distinct from others to which artists have rallied: unlike the plethora of styles and "isms" that appear throughout the nineteenth and twentieth centuries, arts and crafts, like the arts of the Middle Ages, were

Left: A perspective drawing of Ernest Newton's Fouracre at West Green, Hampshire, by Thomas Hamilton Crawford, 1902.

Above: The design by William Burges for St Mary's, Aldford-cum-Studley, Yorkshire, c. 1872. Watercolour by Axel Naig.

Right: The stained-glass Scene from the Annunciation, *by Edward Burne-Jones, 1860, for St Columba's Church, Topcliffe, Yorkshire.*

projected once again into a public rather than a private arena.

SOCIAL PURPOSE

The real nature of the Arts and Crafts Movement was one of social purpose rather than style. This is worth remembering in an age when the outward signs of the movement – its picturesque qualities, its taste for a pastoral idyll and the handcrafted – have made the movement very popular again. The Arts and

Crafts Movement finds its true spirit repeated not in Post-Modernist building in homely brick rather than aggressive concrete, or in the pastoral reminiscences of long-dead Edwardian amateurs, or in the romanticism of fashion houses or advertising agencies that trade in resonant ideals of a picturesque countryside, but in the political, social and cultural bulwarks against the age of 'Gradrind', an age that is by no means limited to either the nineteenth century or England.

THE EVOLUTION OF THE ARTS AND CRAFTS MOVEMENT

The Arts and Crafts Movement evolved and developed during the second half of the nineteenth century. It incorporated a wide variety of artists, writers, craftsmen and -women, so wide that it is difficult to define 'Arts and Crafts' with any accuracy. One has only to consider that some of its precursors were deeply conservative and looked wistfully back to a medieval past, while others were socialists and ardent reformers. Some, like John Ruskin (1819–1900), identified the Arts and Crafts aesthetic with Protestantism, while others, such as the architect A W N Pugin (1812–52), saw clear affinities between the revival of medievalism and the Catholic cause. Moreover, the craftsmen and -women connected with the movement were active within a wide cross-section of crafts: as architects, printers and bookbinders, potters, jewellers, painters, sculptors and cabinetmakers. Some members of the movement, such as the designers William Morris (1834–96) and C R Ashbee (1863–1942), cherished handicraft and tended to reject the opportunity to produce for a mass market. Others, such as the architect Frank Lloyd Wright (1867–1959),

positively relished the creative and social advantages of machine production.

THE SPREAD OF THE ARTS AND CRAFTS MOVEMENT

The Arts and Crafts Movement became even more diverse during the 1870s, when the revival of an interest in the arts and crafts in Britain was exported and grafted onto indigenous traditions abroad. In the United States, the revival of craft traditions had a resonant appeal to a nation with a strong political affinity with individualism and for things handmade and homespun. It is interesting to note that decades before such critics as Thomas Carlyle (1795–1881) or Ruskin were writing about the horror of industrialism and the idyll of rural medieval England, Shaker communities in the United States were producing simple furniture and buildings that echoed many of the creative and social ideals of the Arts and Crafts Movement. Friedrich Engels (1820–95) dissociated himself from the religious faith of the Shakers but admired the near-socialist conditions under which their work was produced and sold.

ARTS AND CRAFTS PRINCIPLES

The revival of arts and crafts in the second half of the nineteenth century embodied a rich and varied tradition of political, religious and aesthetic ideas that found form in a variety of media, yet there were some principles and articles of faith common to the Arts and Crafts Movement in general. The belief that a well-designed environment – fashioned with beautiful and well-crafted buildings, furniture, tapestries and ceramics – would serve to improve the fabric of society for both producers and consumers is a theme common to the Arts and Crafts Movement in both the

Above: An example of the work of the Kelmscott Press, 1896.

Below: Morris' 'Trellis' wallpaper, 1862.

nineteenth and twentieth centuries. The idea was expressed by William Morris in the middle of the nineteenth century and repeated constantly thereafter by kindred spirits in Europe and the United States.

WORKING CONDITIONS

Together with the idea that the material and moral fabric of society were connected, there existed an interest in the working conditions under which the artefacts were produced. A building or piece of furniture, according to the aims of the Arts and Crafts tradition, had not only to be beautiful but also to be the result of contented labour, in which the craftsman or -woman could reject the drudgery and alienation of factory work and delight in simple handicraft. The movement's precursors, Carlyle and, more particularly, Ruskin and Morris, had virtually characterised labour as a sacrament. It was through the medium of work, they maintained, that men and women expressed not only their individual creativity but also the essence of their humanity. In his Lectures on Socialism, Morris wrote that 'Art is Man's expression of his joy in Labour', an expression that the pressure of industrialised

Left: Standen, near East Grinstead, Sussex, designed by Philip Webb in 1892 for James Beale, a London solicitor. The house contains work by Morris, W A S Benson and George Jack, together with a number of other employees of Morris & Co.

factory work had rendered impossible. Morris continued: 'Since all persons . . . must produce in some form or other it follows that under our present system most honest men must lead unhappy lives since their work . . . is devoid of pleasure'. Or, put more succinctly, that in Victorian society, as far as Morris was concerned, 'happiness is only possible to artists and thieves'.

THE RETURN TO A GOLDEN AGE

It was the desire to improve both aesthetic standards and working conditions that generated a further article of faith shared by many active within the Arts and Crafts Movement: the belief that the material and moral fabric of society had been infinitely better at some time in the past, be it the England of the Middle Ages or the America of the pioneer age.

The ethos of industrial capitalism demanded production for profit rather than need and had generated shoddily designed goods in the process at the expense of both their aesthetic appeal to consumers and the well-being of the workforce. These miserable conditions were in stark contrast to those of the pre-industrialised past in which, it was generally believed, production took place under far more wholesome conditions. The crafts of medieval society had none of the engine-turned precision of modern industry, but they retained the sense

Right: A photograph of the Hammersmith branch of the Socialist League. Morris is fifth from the right in the second row. May Morris, wearing a light dress, is in the centre of the front row. Jenny Morris is second to the left of her.

Below: An Arts and Crafts table, casket and candlestick.

of humanity that Ruskin so admired. Writing in 'The Nature of Gothic' in the second volume of *The Stones of Venice*, published in 1853, Ruskin insisted that 'You must make either a tool of the creature or a man of him. You cannot make both. Men were not intended to work with the accuracy of tools, to be precise and perfect in all their actions. If you will have that precision out of them, and make their fingers measure degrees like cog-wheels, and their arms strike curves like compasses, you must unhumanise them'.

HUMANITY OVER INDUSTRIALISATION

Pre-industrial society, then, was understood to have retained precisely that element of humanity that industrial capitalism lacked. Men and women were not bound by the relationship of master and wage-slave, based on alienating and mechanised factory labour, but lived as a human community centred upon the workshop, where they were employed in useful and creative tasks. The admiration for some romanticised, pre-industrial Utopia was endemic among nineteenth-century critics of industrialism – so endemic, in fact, that an echo of the sentiment even permeates the *Economic and Philosophical Manuscripts* of Karl Marx (1818–83). Not generally known for his romanticism, Marx found and admired in the working conditions of medieval society 'an intimate and human side' that was resolutely absent in the factory sweatshops of the industrialised nineteenth century.

TRYING TO RESOLVE THE PARADOX

Not all of the ventures that took place under the banner of the Arts and Crafts Movement were an unqualified success. William Morris, towards the end of his life, expressed profound doubt about the real value of his work and maintained that the undeniably beautiful work produced by his company was undertaken only for the wealthy. There were, in turn,

Left: St Peter and St Paul, *a stained-glass window designed by William Morris and Ford Madox Brown, 1865, for Middleton Cheney Church, Northamptonshire.*

Below: The Six-mark Teapot, *by George Du Maurier, from* Punch, *17 July 1880.*

numerous other well-intentioned craft ventures that began with great optimism only to end in bankruptcy. Morris had stumbled on a paradox that affected all evangelistical craftsmen and -women active within the movement in England and the United States: objects made by hand are far more expensive than those made by machine and necessarily exclude the disadvantaged masses for whom they were intended. Ultimately, there came to the Arts and Crafts Movement the realisation that the social reform demanded by many craftsmen and -women could not be achieved by the Arts and Crafts Movement alone, and there was a catalogue of attempts to resolve this paradox.

A HISTORY OF COMPROMISES

In fact, the history of the Arts and Crafts Movement is, in many respects, a history of compromises, and the various attempted solutions to this paradox throughout the evolution of the movement, from the romantic refuge from industrialisation sought by the Pre-Raphaelites and their circle in the mid-nineteenth century to the development of the craft fraternities and sororities on both sides of the Atlantic to the establishment of the European and American design factories in the twentieth century that compromised earlier romantic ideals and came to terms with mechanised industry. Concentrating on the media of glass and pottery, this book illustrates the ideals of the adherents of the Art and Craft Movement as embodied in their work.

Above: Part of a scene depicting the Flight into Egypt, designed by Edward Burne-Jones in collaboration with Morris & Co for St Michael's Church, Brighton.

ARTS AND CRAFTS GLASS

Previous page: A boudoir lamp by Frederick Carder, 1916.

Below: Christ Suffering the Little Children, stained-glass window designed by Edward Burne-Jones in 1862 for the Church of All Saints, Selsey, Gloucestershire.

In berating Victorian craftsmanship, John Ruskin declared that cut glass was barbarous. He preferred blown glass because he liked its plasticity, and since plasticity was a property of glass (which, after all, is a 'liquid') and since Ruskin believed in the honest use of materials, then it had to follow that cut glass was dishonest. He and his followers conflated good design with morality in design.

They evolved a doctrine which stated that one should go for honest structures and forms and truth to materials; then, as now, such phrases were less clear than they sound. For example, if we agree that the properties of glass are that it is a) transparent and b) essentially a liquid, then it follows c) that your forms should reflect these qualities. But the moral imperative is really arbitrary. Ruskin and William Morris, together with the men and women who followed in their wake, persisted with a philosophical error which confused the properties of a material with its qualities. The material has certain properties – glass has ductility, for example. But we provide the qualities: we say whether a form is sinuous or hard, cruel or soft. True, there are always connections to be argued between properties and qualities, but these are not as binding as those who argue for 'truth to materials' like to maintain.

Of course, Ruskin and Morris used morality as an issue in design in another way, from the viewpoint of the craftsman. And here Ruskin had a point in his attack on cut glass.

DANGEROUS WORK

The glass industry was one of the toughest, because even though it was not transformed by mechanisation like textile, garment and metal manufacture, the work was dangerous. The risk of burns was high and inhalation of acid fumes and contact with poisons added

Right: St Philip, *a stained-glass window for St Michael's Church, Waterford, Hertfordshire, by Philip Webb, c. 1876.*

Left: The Angel Musician, *a stained-glass window by Edward Burne-Jones for St Peter and St Paul Church, Cattistock, Dorset, in collaboration with Morris & Co.*

Above: A cameo-glass vase by George Woodall for Richardson & Sons, Staffordshire, England, c. 1890.

Right: An acid-etched base by James Powell and Sons, England, 1913.

to the health risks. Children, who were employed to feed putty powder onto the polishing wheels during the process of polishing cut glass, were at particular risk: the powder contained a mixture of lead and tin oxides and so we can see that Ruskin, viewing the cut glass as a symbol of unnecessary pain, had a right to condemn it.

The Arts and Crafts solution to the unethical work of industry was to put the craftsman in charge of a project from beginning to end by giving him and his team creative autonomy and responsibility for getting the job done in a manner that was both fair to the client and to the craftsman. This, however, is an expensive approach when the trade thrives on competition through price cutting. The Arts and Crafts Movement was always a luxury movement.

TECHNICAL IMPROVEMENTS

Technically, the nineteenth century was a period of improvements in manufacturing

processes in glass. But the most important feature of the age, to which both the Aesthetic Movement and the Arts and Crafts Movement contributed, was the range of decorative methods: apart from cutting and engraving glass, new Victorian techniques included those of cased glass and acid etching. There were important revivals, too, including those of cameo glass and Venetian filigree glass.

COLOUR

Especially in Britain and the United States, there was a great expansion in consumerism because there were more things available for a lot more people to buy. And what makes things attractive to buy? Colour. Roger Dodsworth, a glass historian, notes that by the time of the 1851 Great Exhibition many of the English factories were showing glassworks in a range of colours – oriental blue, rose, ruby, carnelian and pearl opal. Moreover, the American and English factories developed glass in which one colour would shade into another. Naturally, these colours were given creamy, consumer-oriented names – 'Burmese', 'Peach Bloom', 'Amberina'.

PRESS MOULDING

Glass has also been a significant decorative art form in the United States for nearly 200 years. In the 1820s, the Americans invented press moulding, in which glass is pressed into a patterned mould; this process was swiftly developed as a method for producing a wide range of glass artefacts. These were cheap and imitated quite well the more expensive cutglass wares. And then, in 1864, William Leighton developed soda-lime glass, which was clear, like lead glass, but again much cheaper. The combination of soda glass and press moulding made the cheap imitation of cut-glass ware even easier and the cut-glass craft companies fought back by making their patterns so complicated that they could not be imitated. And so by the 1880s America, in particular, was producing cut-glass ware of fantastic elaboration.

PHILIP WEBB

William Morris set up in business with Edward Burne-Jones, Philip Webb and others in 1861. Earlier, Philip Webb had, together

Right: Detail from The Last Judgement, *Edward Burne-Jones, 1876.*

Below: The Sermon on the Mount, *Dante Gabriel Rossetti, 1862.*

Right: Detail from The Last Judgement, *stained-glass window by Edward Burne-Jones, 1876, St Michael and St Mary Magdalene, Easthampstead, Berkshire.*

Opposite: Detail from the south window in the transept of Jesus College Chapel, Cambridge University, 1873, designed by Edward Burne-Jones and made by Morris, Marshall, Faulkner & Co.

with Morris, started designing glass for the Whitefriars Glass House. This company was founded in the late seventeenth century and was taken over in 1835 by James Powell. Around 1860, the company began producing the elegant, plain, well-proportioned glass wares of Webb's designs. These were, naturally, 'hand' blown. It is also worth noting that James Powell and his son produced their own designs; some were based on Venetian patterns and, as the century progressed, there was an Art Nouveau influence. In the archives of the company are botanical and herbal works. Plants – indeed, empirical natural science in general – were a major influence on progressive decorative design during the nineteenth century.

THE INFLUENCE OF THE PRE-RAPHAELITES

The influence and ideas of the Pre-Raphaelites are important in their effect on the later style of Arts and Crafts glass. The Pre-Raphaelite Brotherhood of painters, of whom Dante Gabriel Rossetti was one of the core members, was committed to a close study of nature and it evolved techniques to present clear, sharply focused images. Rossetti, of course, influenced Morris' close friend Edward Burne-Jones, who painted some of the earlier Morris furniture. In 1857 he designed his first stained-glass panel for the Powells at Whitefriars and he was involved in the first stained-glass commission of Morris, Faulkner & Marshall.

As Burne-Jones developed his artistic skills, he grew further away from the close observation of the Pre-Raphaelites and his figures became more expressive, although they showed some of the odd, rubbery, languid quality that characterised Rossetti's painting. Good examples of Burne-Jones' later work

are to be found in the stained-glass windows that he designed for Birmingham Cathedral.

MORRIS, FAULKNER & MARSHALL'S STAINED GLASS

Morris, Faulkner & Marshall produced a large number of stained-glass windows between 1861 and 1875. The general approach of the firm during this period was to allocate the main design of each commission to one of the central designers, with Morris and Webb adding in the decorative background. Morris designed some windows himself; Rossetti did 36; Ford Madox Brown about 130; and the rest were done by Burne-Jones. Stained glass was then big business.

Martin Harrison has described the basic tenet of the Arts and Crafts Movement as far as stained glass was concerned as being a break with the factory-like production lines which the Victorian companies had evolved. The designer was to make or supervise the making of each stage. The other characteristics are a predilection for Pre-Raphaelite-style figures that combine monumentality with languidness; and plant-form backgrounds from Morris.

HENRY HOLIDAY

Many nineteenth-century artists were influenced by the Pre-Raphaelites and many were swayed by Ruskin and Morris, yet among them were those who had reservations about Morris' commitment to the designs of the medieval craftsman. One of those people was Henry Holiday.

Holiday had studied at the Royal Academy Schools, was influenced by Pre-Raphaelite painters and worked with the architect and designer William Burges. He took over from Burne-Jones at Whitefriars and then started his own stained-glass studio in 1891.

Above: St Matthew, *stained-glass window designed by William Morris, 1862, Christchurch, Southgate, Middlesex.*

Right: The Brachet Licking Sir Tristram, *stained-glass window designed by William Morris, 1861, one of a series of panels illustrating the story of Sir Tristram, made in 1862 for Harden Grange, near Bingley, West Yorkshire, the home of Walter Dunlop, a Bradford merchant.*

Twenty years before, Holiday had argued strongly that artists, designers and architects had to acknowledge the times they were living in. Modernism – above all, science – would not go away, however much one longed for the security of medieval order. He said 'We cannot put on thirteenth-century sentiment . . . When a medieval artist drew the Creator standing upon the earth planting the sun and moon in the heavens, one with each hand, the conception was colossal. But we cannot do this now. Our heads are full of diagrams of the solar system . . . our work is to discover that which is truest and best in our age . . .' Holiday had grasped what Morris had put to one side: the need to find an aesthetic and a content that was appropriate to modern times.

WALTER CRANE AND CHRISTOPHER WHALL
One of the most active propagandists of the

Arts and Crafts Movement was Walter Crane, the first president of the Arts and Crafts Exhibition Society founded in 1888. Crane, like Morris, was an active socialist and did some stained-glass work. One acerbic assessment of his work is that he was a wispy follower of Morris tinged with Art Nouveau.

According to students of the period, however, the leader of the Arts and Crafts Movement, as far as stained glass is concerned, was Christopher Whall, who began as a painter. In his first ventures into stained glass in 1879, Whall was appalled by the way in which his designs were translated for the medium. He set up a small workshop of his own in which he trained a number of important artist/designers, such as Louis Davis and Reginald Hallward. He also lectured on stained glass at the Central School of Arts and Crafts in London and wrote what was considered until recently to be the standard text on the subject: *Stained Glass Work*.

In accordance with the empirical spirit of the times, Whall urged designers to draw from life and from the model. He was highly critical of stylised figures and critical also of the practice of using the same cartoon over and over again in one design after another.

CHRISTOPHER DRESSER AND CHARLES RENNIE MACKINTOSH

With a few exceptions, Arts and Crafts decorated glass, especially stained glass, did not find a modern voice in Britain. Two of these exceptions were Christopher Dresser and Charles Rennie Mackintosh. Dresser began

Right: Detail of angels from a stained-glass window designed by William Morris, 1873, St Peter and St Paul, Over Stowey, Somerset.

lecturing on botany in 1854. He became a designer and in 1876 set up Dresser and Holme, a company importing oriental wares. In the 1890s, having by then been design director for the Linthorpe Pottery, as well as a designer for Minton and the author of, among other works, *Modern Ornamentation*, he designed glass for James Couper & Sons of Glasgow. His simple, relatively plain, glass volumes are functionalist and modern (they anticipate the Bauhaus aesthetic); their geometry is tempered with a grace that comes from an understanding of the fluid nature of glass.

Dresser made a vital contribution to design in glassware, partly because he was not hemmed in by an ideology that was frightened of the machine or machine production. In glass, he provided an intelligent, modern bridge between the enlightened historicism of Morris and the new age. He designed with modern production methods in mind, which meant acknowledging the division of labour within a framework of pre-determined production sequences.

Mackintosh, who trained as an architect, was attracted to Art Nouveau decoration, which he developed into a particularly abstract form. Indeed, his abstraction was criticised when he showed some of his designs at the fifth exhibition of the Arts and Crafts Exhibition Society in 1896.

The rectilinear style developed by Mackintosh, in company with the designers H J MacNair and Margaret and Frances Macdonald, proved influential, especially in Austria. There was also a reciprocity of aesthetics between Mackintosh's glass designs (as seen in the Willow Tea Rooms in Glasgow) and the contemporary work of Frank Lloyd Wright. The most direct interchange of influence, however, was between Mackintosh and Vienna: designers such as Koloman Moser and Josef Hoffmann were much impressed by what was happening in Glasgow.

THE VIENNA SECESSION

At the turn of the century, the Vienna Secession, the group of Austrian artists and architects which had broken away from the established academy to found its own organisation, began exhibiting its own work and that of foreigners such as Mackintosh. The writ of Ruskin and Morris held firm for Secessionists such as Hoffmann, who, with Moser, had helped to establish the art-craft workshop co-operative the Wiener Werkstätte. Hoffmann stated that the aim of those

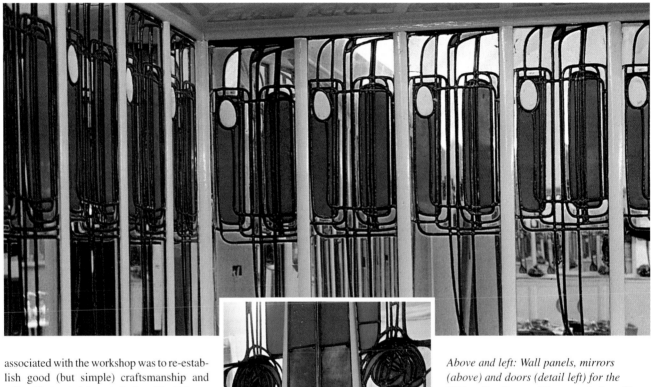

associated with the workshop was to re-establish good (but simple) craftsmanship and refined but not elaborate design. The Wiener Werkstätte produced glass which was manufactured by glass companies in Bohemia. As the twentieth century progressed, the Secessionist glass designs became more and more geometric and architectural in their form.

AMERICAN ARTS AND CRAFTS GLASS
The nineteenth century, dominated as it was by trade, saw an increase in the number of international exhibitions which, together with magazines, spread ideas from one country to another rapidly. American technology was soon superior to European technology, but the styles were Eurocentric, partly because

Above and left: Wall panels, mirrors (above) and doors (detail left) for the Willow Tea Rooms, Glasgow, designed by Charles Rennie Mackintosh, 1904.

Below: A collection of Loetz iridescent glass, Austria, c. 1900.

Opposite: The Tiffany "Poppy'"lamp, U.S.A., c. 1900.

many immigrants were European and also because travel, especially by the children of the new Americans, to Europe, was popular.

JOHN LA FARGE

One of the American glass painters who was initially close to the British Arts and Crafts Movement was John La Farge, who, as well as having been taught by his father, a fresco painter, studied in Paris. He was, for a while, influenced by the Pre-Raphaelites, but was

especially impressed by the flat pattern-making approach to decoration developed by Morris. However, during the 1890s, he developed a much more figural and naturalistic content. La Farge patented a method for producing opalescent glass in 1880 (Louis Comfort Tiffany also developed a similar process independently in 1881). La Farge had a number of major clients, including such millionaire families as the Vanderbilts and the Whitneys, who collected his work.

Above: A Tiffany 'Jack-in-the-Pulpit' vase, USA, c. 1900.

FRANK LLOYD WRIGHT

British arts and crafts were shown at the Centennial Exposition in Philadelphia in 1876 and the work displayed included items from Morris, Crane and Fairfax Murray. Later in the century, both Crane and Ashbee began to visit and lecture throughout America and both became friends of Frank Lloyd Wright, himself a founder member of the Chicago Arts and Crafts Society set up in 1897.

Wright admired both Ruskin and Morris but made it clear that he was not antagonistic towards the machine. Indeed, his rectilinear designs for glass show an imagination which sees the machine and its precision and rationality as sources for metaphor and symbolism and thus a cause for celebration. Wright's imagination was, even more than Dresser's, a natural conduit between Arts and Crafts design and the machine age. His aesthetic began with organic or botanical forms but moved towards a geometrical order. His leaded glass, as seen in Darwin D Martin's house in Buffalo, for example, shows an aesthetic which has turned the attenuations of Art Nouveau line into a formal arrangement of squares and rectangles.

LOUIS COMFORT TIFFANY

With regard to Art Nouveau and Arts and Crafts in American glass, the most notable practitioner is Louis Comfort Tiffany, who claimed to be influenced by Morris. He had the splendid idea of running a quasi-Italian Renaissance workshop: he would be the master, with a plenitude of assistants, and his ambition was to improve industrial design by injecting art into it. He also wanted to raise the standards of design for items used in the home. These aims paralleled those of Morris.

He parallels Morris in another way. Morris had a genius for pattern and, in particular, for making decorative use of flowers and plants, but on flat, two-dimensional surfaces. Tiffany shared the same ability to compose with nature but he could do it three-dimensionally, like a sculptor. He made his glass and metalware mimic the plasticity of drooping plants and entwining tendrils. He had started in stained glass in the early 1870s and founded the Tiffany Furnaces in 1892. In 1895 he showed a collection of stained-glass windows which had been designed by a number of French painters, including Pierre Bonnard, Edouard Vuillard and Henri de Toulouse Lautrec.

Tiffany was an eclectic: he had travelled in Spain and North Africa; he was excited by the exotic; and his personal triumph was the patenting of handmade, iridescent glass which he called 'Favrile'. It proved immensely popular. The exotic, warm-coloured lamps which he produced were highly successful and the Tiffany style, a golden or red-blood, womb-like excess, has continued to appeal to Western consumers and has also been much copied.

FREDERICK CARDER

Tiffany had rivals, and one of the fiercest was Frederick Carder, who worked first in England (he was born in Staffordshire) and left in 1903 to found the Steuben Glass works in Corning, New York. Carder was the designer and he developed a range of iridescent and metalicised glassware to compete with Tiffany's.

ARTS AND CRAFTS IN SCANDINAVIA

Elsewhere in the world, in Scandinavia especially, the British Arts and Crafts Movement was particularly influential. In Sweden, Ellen Key published a book, called *Beauty for All*, inspired by Morris' writings. The emphasis on social democracy in Sweden and the interest

Left: A collection of Tiffany iridescent glass vases, USA, c. 1900.

in creating a humane environment in sympathy both with nature and the need to make life comfortable made the Arts and Crafts ideology, with its concentration upon the home, an appropriate one.

The Scandinavians were not swamped by the ideology of 'the machine'; none of its nations underwent an industrial revolution that was remotely equivalent to those seen in Britain, the United States and Germany.

Whereas the industrial landscape of Britain, for example, had led British designers and craftsmen to take an elaborate and forced view of natural decoration in their work in order to emphasise their ideological embrace of nature and their rejection of the machine, in Sweden the tension between industry and nature was nothing like so acute. For one thing, the natural landscape of the country was still intact.

ANNA BOBERG

Take, for example, the work of Anna Boberg, of Sweden's Rijmyre Glassworks, the wife of the architect and designer Ferdinand Boberg. The characteristic of her work was the juxtaposition of abstract and natural designs, a balancing of nature and art which captures the essence of the Swedish landscape.

GUNNAR WENNERBERG

Although he is known primarily as a ceramics designer, Gunnar Wennerberg was one of the best Swedish glass designers. He did much of his work for the Kosta factory and created overlay glass inspired by Emile Gallé, the highly talented French glass-maker and doyen of Art Nouveau. Overlay glass consists of a core covered with one or more layers of glass in different colours, wheel-cut or etched through these layers to produce a raised pattern of colour that contrasts with the ground. Wennerberg was also interested in the rendering of surfaces to make compositions of different textures.

THE ARTS AND CRAFTS LEGACY IN GLASS

By the end of the nineteenth century one of the virtues of Art Nouveau, from the Arts and Crafts point of view, was that it appeared to put craftsmanship and decorative art on a footing with other arts. In fact, the craftsmen were fooling themselves: the avant-garde in painting and sculpture was already, via Impressionism and Post-Impressionism, in the act of deskilling itself. This rejection of skill continued throughout the twentieth century. Yet the middle classes have consistently preferred the bourgeois decorative arts to the full-blooded imagery of Modernism. Glass in particular has remained a minor, although delightful, art, reflecting middlebrow sensibilities, whatever its form or setting.

Right: St Cecilia, *stained-glass panel designed by Edward Burne-Jones, about 1872–73, made by Morris & Co in about 1897.*

BRITISH POTTERY

Previous page: Baluster vase by Mark V Marshall for Doulton, London, c. 1910.

Pottery was among the most handsome, well-crafted and innovative of the vast and variegated output of Arts and Crafts designers, from sturdy, lustre-painted earthenware to delicate, crystalline-glazed porcelain. It was copiously copied, using a wide variety of techniques, decorated with an extensive range of colourful paints, enamels and glazes and was enhanced further with subjects ranging from fantastic, medieval beasts and doughty Viking sailing ships to exquisite pendant wistaria and noble Native American chiefs.

Below right: Pot with lid, made by Charles Cox at the Mortlake Pottery, 1912.

Even the forms were diverse and at times outrageous: a menagerie of moon-faced jugs and bird-shaped tobacco jars from London's eccentric Martin brothers; an array of crumpled, crinkled and convoluted vases by George Ohr of Mississippi; a series of square earthenware tiles painted with a verdant arrangement of tendrils and blooms by William De Morgan to a William Morris design; and the 'Scarab' vase, an award-winning, massive, lattice-worked extravagance from the American Adelaide Alsop Robinson.

The growth of art pottery in Britain, as in the United States, was stupendous: not only were newly founded potteries creating outstanding and popular vessels, but long-established factories either started creative art-pottery divisions producing lovely works in small quantities, or else marketed wares designed by prominent craft-revival artist/designers.

THE BRITISH POTTERY-MAKING TRADITION
The making of pottery and porcelain had long been an important enterprise in Britain – in Staffordshire and Derbyshire, especially – so it is only natural that Arts and Crafts potters built on, and greatly added to, this firm foundation. Many of the techniques used by

mid-nineteenth-century British potteries were not at all shoddy or second-rate, as in other mass-production media, and their products proved both influential and attractive to other British potters, as well as to Americans.

There was also a growing interest in older production and decoration methods, many of these allowing individuals within large studio situations to design, throw, fire and paint their wares – that is, to control the entire creative process from start to finish. At the same time, there was an increase in creative teamwork, in keeping with Arts and Crafts tenets whereby, for instance, a vase or charger came to exist through the joint efforts of a skilled potter, who threw and fired the vessel, and an equally talented painter, who decorated it according to the design of still a third person, perhaps a well-known illustrator.

WILLIAM FREND DE MORGAN

The London-born William Frend De Morgan was associated with William Morris' firm from 1863, designing both tiles and stained glass, and in 1872 he founded his own pottery and showroom in Chelsea. At first he painted ready-made blank tiles and vessels, primarily utilising two techniques, lustre and enamel. In the early Chelsea period, from 1872 to 1882, his subject matter was rather eclectic: tiles and dishes decorated with somewhat laboured, neo-classical designs, such as *putti,* scrolls and palmettes, with Morris-inspired, stylised blossoms and tendrils, or with a bestiary full of creatures, both playful and monstrous, often executed in shimmering lustre tones of red, yellow, pink, silver and gold.

The metallic film decorating these lustre pieces was much used on the designs of two De Morgan employees, Charles and Frederick Passenger, and also sparked their imitation by

other potteries. They were created in part because of De Morgan's admiration of Italian maiolica from Gubbio, the ruby lustreware of which was especially vibrant. But De Morgan expanded his palette further, around 1875, adding to his repertory the so-called 'Persian' colours – rich, deep shades of turquoise and royal blue, red, yellow, violet and green (often with black on white slip grounds).

Between 1882 and 1888 De Morgan flourished at a new, purpose-built pottery at Merton Abbey, close to Morris' works; the two men

Above: An earthenware painted dish with peacock motif by William De Morgan.

sometimes collaborated on tile projects, Morris doing the designing and De Morgan producing and decorating. In 1888, he set up a new factory in Sands End, Fulham, with Halsey Ricardo, an architect, as his partner. The pair worked together until 1898, a decade considered to be De Morgan's richest and most successful period.

Because of failing health, De Morgan had begun to spend time in Italy, where he established a studio in Florence, providing designs for his own firm and for the Italian pottery Cantagalli. In 1898, the two Passenger brothers became partners, as did also his kilnmaster, Frank Iles. De Morgan himself stopped producing pottery in 1907 and turned to writing novels, but his three partners kept the firm running until 1911.

DE MORGAN'S WORK

Along with the Passengers and a talented artist, Joe Juster, among others, De Morgan produced lustred and enamelled earthenware of increasing beauty and technical virtuosity, especially in the early Fulham years. He made his own blanks at Merton Abbey – tiles, as well as dishes, bowls, vases and bottles – and some of their forms, clearly oriental in inspiration, were especially attractive. Besides the plant, flower and animal designs which his wares featured, De Morgan also favoured a beloved Arts and Crafts motif: the sturdy Viking sailing ship, usually a richly ornamented galleon on a glittering sea of stylised waves. Individual art tiles and panels were always a mainstay of De Morgan's production. His botanical, zoological and maritime designs were presented alone, in pairs or even

Right: A series of underglazed earthenware tiles by William De Morgan.

as parts of 'four-square' designs on single tiles; sometimes they formed a running design or a large pictorial composition.

THE MARTIN BROTHERS

From the kilns of the four eccentric Martin brothers – Robert Wallace, Charles Douglas, Walter Frazier and Edwin Bruce – came some of the most renowned and unusual art pottery of all: salt-glazed stoneware which, among other creatures, took the forms of chubby-jowled, wide-nosed, two-faced jugs and leering or sneering anthropomorphic bird jars. Robert had studied sculpture, exhibiting from around 1863, but by 1871 he had turned to creating stoneware, first working with Jean-Charles Cazin at the Fulham Pottery, and two years later setting up a studio with his brothers in the King's Road, Fulham. Charles handled the financial and retail ends of the business (a shop near High Holborn was opened in 1879), while Robert was the modeller, Walter the chief thrower and firer and Edwin the chief painter and decorator.

MARTINWARE

In 1877 the partnership moved to Southall, Middlesex, and until 1914 the three creative Martins produced an extensive body of functional and/or decorative pieces, from stoneware vases and jugs to toothpick holders and spoon-warmers. Salt-glazed in shades of cream, brown, grey, blue and green for the most part, quintessential Martinware took the form of semi-real or wholly imaginary bipeds or quadrupeds, but conventionally shaped vessels were also made: tiny vases whose textured, earth-toned glazes simulated snakeskin, sea-urchin shell and tree bark; larger jugs or vases sporting incised and painted organic or animal motifs; still others in the shapes of gourds.

The most interesting Martinware pieces were the grotesques, including hybrid-creature jugs with gaping mouths that served as spouts and curling tails as handles; Heckle-and-Jeckle-like birds, whose facial expressions ran the gamut of human emotion and whose postures expressed the full range of 'body language'; and two-faced, globular 'Janus jugs', some with barristers' wigs and sly,

Below: A lug-handled baluster vase painted with stylised motifs in the so-called 'Persian' colours by William De Morgan, c. 1888–98.

Above: An owl-centred charger, c. 1888–98, whose florid border is a stunning example of William De Morgan's metallic lustreware in yellow and ochre pigments.

immensely talented Martins produced their wares for over 30 years, garnering praise from clients who ranged from Dante Gabriel Rossetti to Queen Victoria.

SIR EDMUND ELTON

Some of the Martins' animal-shaped vases were faintly echoed in vases created by Sir Edmund Elton at his Sunflower Pottery in Somerset. A self-educated art potter, the gifted amateur produced his 'Elton ware' from about 1879: boldly shaped, earthenware jugs, jars, bowls and vases made from local clays, often decorated with applied avian and floral motifs of medieval inspiration. By the early 1900s Elton was sheathing his vessels with handsome metallic glazes, his most distinctive bearing a glistening, *craquelé* surface, attained by firing a layer of liquid gold over one of liquid platinum. Some Elton vases sported several applied handles and one jug featured a crackled glaze, a spout in the shape of an open-jawed serpent's head and it also had a tail-like handle.

CHRISTOPHER DRESSER

The botanist, designer and author Christopher Dresser created some outstanding vessels for several pottery firms, mostly in the 1880s and 1890s. Dresser was the main impetus behind the short-lived Linthorpe Pottery in Yorkshire, which he founded in 1879 with the wealthy landowner John Harrison. Linthorpe was managed by Henry Tooth who, in 1882, established the Bretby Art Pottery in Derbyshire with William Ault. Ault in turn started his own eponymously named company in 1887, for which Dresser designed in the 1890s.

Dresser's designs for Linthorpe were influenced largely by various oriental and ancient motifs. Their glazes were generally dark brown

knowing smiles, others with droll, man-in-the-moon grins.

The inspiration for these unique, one-off creatures was partly Darwinian, partly Japanese, partly Victorian Gothic, but always elaborated by the creative, somewhat disturbed, minds of the brothers. Despite a variety of physical and emotional catastrophes that plagued their ill-starred lives, the prolific,

Left: An example of the grotesque birds made by Robert Wallace Martin during the 1890s.

with green, or else solid yellow, blue or green, their forms often of Middle and Far Eastern inspiration. Some of Dresser's creations for Ault are among his best-known designs in any medium. One vase, available with either a buttercup-yellow or deep-turquoise glaze, sports four handles which are fierce monster heads, from which protrude pairs of inward-curving horns. Another has a double-gourd form with four applied handles shaped as goats' heads. Dresser's designs for Minton and Wedgwood were executed in the 1860s and 1870s and, for the most part, consist of traditionally shaped vessels with oriental or other exotic motifs.

WALTER CRANE

From the late 1860s, the artist and designer Walter Crane designed both tiles and pottery for several major firms, including Wedgwood, Minton and Pilkington. For Maw & Co in Shropshire, a tile manufacturer, he designed hand-coloured, transfer-printed tiles, and for Pilkington's so-called 'Lancastrian ware' he created vases, chargers and plaques in the early 1900s, which were painted by Richard Joyce with rich medieval motifs, such as a jousting knight in silver lustre. Another of his designs for Pilkington was a series of six tiles known as 'Flora's Train', each depicting a charming

Right: Three pieces by the Martin brothers of London and Southall. The two-handled vase (1886) features a charming design of daisies and foxgloves against a buff background. The bird-jars, both with detachable heads, are prime specimens from the Martins' stoneware aviary; the leering creature (left) dates from 1891; the hook-beaked flyer is dated 1905.

'flower fairy' clad in a flowing gown and wearing a petalled hat that echo the form and hue of the blossoms gently entwining each of them. Examples of the *cuenca* technique, these moulded earthenware tiles are filled in with colourful glazes, almost like *cloisonné* enamel.

DOULTON & CO

The British potteries hopped on the bandwagon and set up departments or studios devoted to producing wares in the Arts and Crafts manner. Doulton & Co, established in 1815 by John Doulton and located from 1826 in Lambeth, south London, employed craft-revival designers and painters of note, many connected with the Lambeth School of Art, including many women, such as Hannah Barlow and Eliza Simmance. Until the 1860s, Doulton manufactured decorative bottles and flasks and ordinary household jugs and jars, but the alliance with the Lambeth school, under

its headmaster John Sparkes, led to the production of more sophisticated decorated pottery, including porcelain and earthenware. The latter was made at facilities in Burslem, Stoke-on-Trent, where various new glazes were introduced, some imitative of oriental techniques and others of French crystalline ceramic surfaces.

Numerous Arts and Crafts motifs worked their way into the design repertory of both the Burslem and Lambeth works. Out of Lambeth came a wide variety of decorative pieces. At first these were rather heavy-handed histori-cising vases and plaques, but later salt-glazed and faience wares appeared which were highly inventive in terms both of modelling and the manner and subject matter of their decoration. Hannah Barlow and Mary Mitchell produced wares with handsome, incised deco-rations, and Eliza Simmance and Florence Barlow perfected the *pâte-sur-pâte*

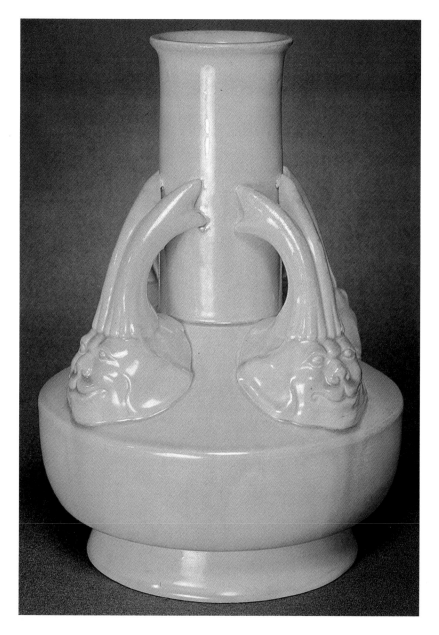

Left: A grotesque vase designed by Christopher Dresser for William Ault, c. 1892.

Above: A Linthorpe bowl designed by Christopher Dresser, c. 1880.

Right: A decorative bowl designed by William Moorcroft.

technique, in which a bas-relief design is effected by applying several layers of slip. Advances in modelling were made by Mark V Marshall and George Tinworth, with handsome, applied elements – lizards, frogs and blossoms – clinging to vases and jugs in a supremely naturalistic manner.

MINTON, WEDGWOOD AND PILKINGTON

Minton's Stoke-on-Trent pottery and porcelain works was another long-established firm which embraced the studio-art movement. Founded in 1793 by Thomas Minton, the Staffordshire company opened Minton's Art-Pottery Studios in South Kensington, London, in 1871, which existed only until 1875. Wares with a distinctive Arts and Crafts bent, however, were produced up to about 1895 at the Staffordshire factory.

Two other solid old firms, Josiah Wedgwood & Sons (established in 1759 in Burslem) and Pilkington's Tile & Pottery Co (founded in Lancashire in 1892) produced Arts and Crafts-style wares. Pilkington made tiles to designs by Walter Crane, C F A Voysey and Lewis F Day, and in 1902 it added lustreware known as 'Royal Lancastrian' to its extensive output. Rich Arts and Crafts motifs, such as knights fighting dragons and proud peacocks, figured on this line, and among the company's gifted painters were Gordon M Forsyth, Gwladys Rogers and Richard Joyce.

Wedgwood, in 1903, forged a 30-year-long relationship with the designer/decorator Alfred H Powel, who had exhibited at the Arts and Crafts Exhibition Society with his wife

Louise. The couple also produced painted earthenware at their own potteries. One of Alfred's most handsome vases for Wedgwood, made in 1920, is covered with a brightly painted medieval landscape on a cream-coloured earthenware ground. Although its date is somewhat late, its motif and sentiment clearly and lovingly hark back to the 1860s and 1870s.

THE DELLA ROBBIA POTTERY

After William De Morgan's firm, the one organised most along Arts and Crafts guide-lines was the Della Robbia Pottery, established in Birkenhead in 1894. Its co-founders were the painter and poet Harold Rathbone and Conrad Dressler, a sculptor who was largely responsible for Della Robbia's architectural commissions. The company was formed to produce architectural decorations, but colourful and attractive utilitarian pieces soon formed a significant part of its output.

Rathbone was strongly averse to repetition and perfection in his works, preferring each piece to be judged on its own. He was equally determined that his employees use their talents to the fullest, expressing their own ideas and enjoying their work. For the 12 years of its

Below left: A vase by William Moorcroft, Cobridge, Staffordshire, c. 1916. Moorcroft produced this popular pattern for years, ever brightening its palette and smoothing down its surface. The toadstool motif appeared on Moorcroft's wares until the 1930s.

Below: A 'Florian-ware' vase by William Moorcroft for James A Macintyre, Burslem, c. 1902. In strong and muted shades of blue on a white ground, the vase features a lovely landscape outlined in high-relif slip.

Right: An example of early twentieth-century glazed ware from the Ruskin Factory, Birmingham.

existence, the Della Robbia Pottery produced a diverse body of functional and decorative hollow-ware and architectural elements.

Various decorating methods were employed, among them painting, applied relief and moulding, but a conventional maiolica technique was the most common (lead glazes applied over a white slip). Rathbone further demanded that an incised (or *sgraffito*) outline be scratched onto each piece to delineate which sections were to receive the glaze. Colours were rich and lustrous, a pale-blue-green being the predominant hue, with bright yellows, reds and oranges, black, cream and other shades of blue and green being common. Decorative motifs included Renaissance-style portraits, Celtic interlace, Islamic and heraldic patterns, floral and foliate designs, even grotesque creatures; forms ranged from round plaques and platters to rectangular clock cases to a fish-shaped spoon-warmer.

WILLIAM MOORCROFT

A more commercially successful venture than Della Robbia was begun in 1913 by William A Moorcroft, a Staffordshire potter who had been associated with James A Macintyre & Co at Burslem from 1897 until he started his own pottery at Cobridge. His art-pottery line for Macintyre, 'Florian ware' (introduced in 1898 and made until around 1904), proved highly successful and provided the basis for many of his own later Cobridge designs.

Moorcroft's wares were very much his personal product: he developed them, designed their shapes and decorations and oversaw those who actually worked with the clay and paint. His name is today most identified with the handsome, distinctive designs that cover his expertly shaped pieces. From early wares with a high-relief slip outline to later works with smooth, shiny surfaces, his firm designing hand can be clearly discerned. The floral patterns – of poppies, lilacs, cornflowers, violets – adorning Florian ware were sometimes busy and overstylised, but after 1904 the blossoms became more softly muted, more at one with their backgrounds, whether white or coloured. Among the non-floral designs, the stylised peacock feather

Right: Nine pieces by the Ruskin Pottery, Birmingham. The pottery was renowned for its flambé *glazes, fired onto vessels at a high temperature. This group shows the variety of colours and shapes, most of the latter of oriental inspiration.*

was one that was especially attractive.

One of Moorcroft's best-known patterns, the 'Hazledene' tall trees in a landscape, was introduced in 1902 and remained popular throughout the 1920s. Two other of his famous patterns, 'Claremont', with its bold, colourful toadstools, and 'Pomegranate', originated in the late Macintyre period and were produced into the 1930s, when the Moorcroft palette (which now included rich *flambé* glazes) was rife with lustrous greens, reds, oranges and yellows, often against a characteristic deep-blue ground. Moorcroft's forms ranged from baluster and waisted vases and classically shaped ewers and tazzas to elaborately lidded *bonbonnières* and architectonic clock cases.

'TORQUAY POTTERY'

The wares of several south Devon potteries producing so-called 'Torquay pottery' from around 1870 were handmade from local clay in the Arts and Crafts manner and were decorated with paints and glazes also made locally, if not on the premises. These included the Watcombe Pottery, the Aller Vale Pottery and the Long Park Pottery.

THE RUSKIN POTTERY

Another small firm, the Ruskin Pottery, was established in 1898 in Birmingham by Edward Richard Taylor and his son, William Howson Taylor. Its output was acclaimed for its extensive range of handsome, *flambé* glazes. Fired at extremely high temperatures, the vessels often gleamed with breathtaking combinations of mottled hues, both strong and muted, these were enhanced by stunning, stippled effects resulting from the use of copper salts; lustre glazes, too, were employed.

Right: A 'Barum-ware' blue-glazed earthen-ware jug in the shape of a bird by Charles H Brannum, Barnstaple, north Devon, c. 1879. Prior to this art-pottery line Brannum made ovens and kitchenware.

BRANNUM, THE FOLEY POTTERY AND THE OMEGA WORKSHOPS

From 1879 the Barnstaple, north Devon pottery of Charles H Brannum produced a line of art pottery known as 'Barum ware' – simply shaped vases and jugs decorated with flowers, animals and other devices in coloured slip on white ground; later pieces were moulded in avian and other creatures' shapes.

Another noted pottery was the Foley Pottery, a Staffordshire porcelain manufacturer. In the 1930s Foley commissioned designs from such painters as Duncan Grant and Vanessa Bell, whose own Omega Workshops created distinctive art pottery. The workshops' director, Roger Fry, and his colleagues were determined to show the public the advantages of decoration by artists of quotidian objects, including pottery vessels, most of which were made at Harold Stabler's Poole Pottery in Dorset.

LIBERTY & CO

There existed dozens of smaller firms which also created wares in the Arts and Crafts manner. Many of these wares were sold at Liberty, the London retail emporium which offered well-crafted, but generally mass-produced, objects to an eager public. Among the various art-pottery lines that Liberty stocked were Burmantoft's Faience, Barum ware, Pilkington's Royal Lancastrian, William Moorcroft's Florian ware, Royal Doulton and the designs of the Bretby, Aller Vale, Foley, Poole, Farnham and Della Robbia potteries.

AMERICAN AND CONTINENTAL POTTERY

Previous page: An earthenware dish produced at Valby, Denmark, by Thorvald Bindesbøll, 1901.

Below right: A Rookwood earthenware jar with coloured underglazes, decorated by Hattie E Wilcox, 1900.

In the United States, the halcyon days of art pottery encompassed the period from approximately 1870 to 1930. Not only were vessels such as vases, cups, bowls, chargers and *jardinières* produced in endless varieties and huge quantities, but there was also a boom in art-tile production. These objects were at times more sophisticated and innovative in style, technique and decoration than their European counterparts, although they were, of course, greatly indebted to them.

While some American potteries found success in a matter of years, others failed in just as brief a time or were taken over by other firms; only a handful lasted for more than a decade or two.

MARY LOUISE MCLAUGHLIN

The history begins in Cincinnati, Ohio, where in 1873 Mary Louise McLaughlin, a daughter of that city's foremost architect, took a popular class in china painting at the local school of design. By 1876 she was exhibiting her overglaze-decorated wares at the Centennial Exposition in Philadelphia and in 1879 she organised the Cincinnati Pottery Club (sometimes called the Women's Pottery Club). One of the local women whom she invited to join her group was Maria Longworth Nichols, who, in 1880, started her own pottery. Called Rookwood, it would become America's foremost maker of art pottery.

McLaughlin's career, which lasted only until about 1904, was neither as long nor as commercially successful as Nichols', but her contribution to the creative atmosphere that enveloped china-mad Cincinnati cannot be overemphasised. Although her underglaze-slip wares, called 'Cincinnati Limoges' because of their resemblance to the French porcelain, were expertly executed and attractively decorated with lush floral scenes, they were ultimately less decorative and sold less well than Rookwood's later wares. In the early 1880s McLaughlin decorated some Rookwood-thrown and -fired pieces in under-glaze paint, but in 1883 she became involved instead in other pursuits. In 1898, however, she returned to pottery-making, experimenting with hard-paste porcelains that she called 'Losanti ware'. At first, she painted decorations on these pieces and later turned to carved floriate and foliate motifs, which had pale glaze colours in the Art Nouveau vein. Although her career was far from the financial success that Nichols' was, of the two she remained the experimenter and the stalwart individual artist potter.

MARIA LONGWORTH NICHOLS

Maria Longworth Nichols (later Storer) first came into contact with pottery via Karl Langenbeck, a ceramics chemist, with whom she carried on china-painting experiments in 1871. Highly ambitious, she turned what had started out as a mere hobby into a thriving business. Soon after establishing her Rookwood Pottery, she was employing a talented group of men (who did the throwing and firing, as well as the decorating) and women (decorators, in the main) and was producing a line of handsome glazed wares.

One employee, Laura A Fry, is credited with inventing an ingenious atomiser method for spraying coloured slips onto the green, wet, clay body, achieving a smooth finish on which several colours could be laid and relief-slip design applied. Fry's technique was used for the so-called 'standard'-glazed Rookwood pieces, which often featured *japoniste* floral and insect designs on green, yellow, amber and taupe grounds.

Left: A Rookwood vase which was exhibited at the Paris Exhibition of 1900.

Right: Of all its wares, Rookwood's vases are among the best known; this one is decorated with a bird and foliage.

ROOKWOOD PIECES

Various other glazes and lines were introduced in subsequent years – the cool 'Sea Green', the pastel-dominated 'Iris' and several matte types (including 'Vellum'). Besides classically shaped vessels, Rookwood produced pieces which bore a resemblance to such organic forms as gourds and lotuses. Another speciality was a flat, rectangular plaque, usually painted with a 'Vellum'-glaze landscape, a hazily Impressionistic mountain scene, perhaps, or a grey-green Tonalist river view. In addition to highly popular depictions of nature – floral sprays, landscapes, fish, birds and even bats in flight – there were also vases painted with portraits of noble Native Americans, these for the most part by one of Rookwood's finest decorators, Matthew A Daly, in sombre tones against an amber standard glaze. Other decorators included Albert R Valentien, Carl Schmidt, Kataro Shirayamadani, Harriet E Wilcox and Artus Van Briggle, who later started his own pottery in Colorado Springs.

Rookwood pieces were occasionally embellished further with silver: a mug of 1898 was painted with brown-green hops by Sara Sax and capped with a silver collar by Reed & Barton of Taunton, Massachusetts; and an elaborate, trumpet-necked vase was overlaid with a chased-silver floral mount by Gorham Manufacturing Co of Providence, Rhode Island. Many pieces made between 1905 and 1915 were decorated with monochromatic, earth-toned matte glazes. Stylised floral forms and common Arts and Crafts motifs, such as the peacock feather, were used on these solid, handsome wares.

THE WELLER POTTERY

Other potteries sprouted in and around Cincinnati during Rookwood's heyday, including the Avon Pottery, T J Wheatley and Co and the Lonhuda Pottery, opened by William A Long in 1892 in Steubenville, Ohio, which was bought by Samuel A Weller, who ran a commercial ceramics factory in Zanesville, Ohio. As the Weller Pottery, it became a significant force in American art pottery, as did Zanesville ('Clay City') itself. In addition to producing traditionally shaped

Below: A Rookwood tile, featuring a pair of rabbits flanking a tulip tree. It was made in 1911 and has a high-gloss glaze rather than the matte finish usually employed by Rookwood.

Right: A bowl by Frederick Hurton Rhead at Rhead Pottery, Santa Barbara, California, c. 1915. He used an inlaid process and an Egyptian scarab motif.

wares with painted underglaze decoration, Weller moulded some of his pots with leaf and insect designs, covering the whole piece in solid green, blue or brown matte glaze. He also hired Jacques Sicard, and the talented Frenchman's 'Sicardo ware' – lovely, lustre, floral designs on iridescent grounds of amber, green and aubergine – transformed standard Weller vessels into shimmering confections.

THE ROSEVILLE POTTERY

Frederick Hurten Rhead, a British-born ceramics designer, also worked for Weller from 1902 to 1904, creating several lines characterised by stylised natural forms. Rhead's best-known undertaking, however, was the art directorship of Zanesville's Roseville Pottery, established by George F Young in 1892. The company's first art-pottery line, known as

Left: A tile by Arthur Osborne for the Low Art Tile Works of Chelsea, Massachusetts, c. 1880. Osborne designed this long, vertical tile of a shepherd and his dog and flock using the clouded, or pooled, glaze effect characteristic of many Low tiles; it was obtained by allowing the glaze to collect in the tile's crevices.

Above: A tile by Grueby Faience Company, Boston, c. 1905. Grueby created hand-decorated tiles, like this square, featuring a vintage galleon.

'Rozane', was hand-painted on slip on a dark ground and then brightly glazed; later wares were covered with matte glazes and often featured moulded floral and leaf decorations. Immensely prolific, Roseville managed to produce its popular, relatively inexpensive wares until 1954.

OTHER POTTERIES

In Ohio, other noted potteries were J B Owens' operation and the Mosaic Tile Company, while other Midwestern potteries included the Overbeck Pottery in Indiana and Pewabic in Detroit, Michigan. In the Chicago area, the Gates Potteries of Terra Cotta, Illinois, produced a line of green-glazed art pottery from 1900 called 'Teco', which was often designed by sculptors and architects (at least one piece by Frank Lloyd Wright).

THE GRUEBY FAIENCE CO

The Boston area was especially rich in potteries, including the Chelsea Keramic Art Works and the Chelsea Pottery, the Grueby Faience Co being its most prominent. William H Grueby had worked at the tile-maker J and J G Low, in Chelsea, Massachusetts, before establishing his own firm in east Boston in 1894. From around 1898, the majority of his vessels and tiles were covered with distinctive glazes; they came in shades of yellow, blue, mauve and brown, but the dark-green hue, with a mottled effect like that on a watermelon rind, was by far the best known and soon the most imitated. The thick-walled, faintly organic vessels – highlighted with moulded veining and floral and foliate elements, sometimes in another colour – were beautifully proportioned, simply decorated and subtly hued masterworks. Most were designed by George P Kendrick, thrown at a wheel and finally decorated by one of a number of talented women painters, including Ruth Erickson and Lillian Newman.

Grueby also manufactured architectural tiles. Mostly hand-decorated, these tiles – sometimes single, sometimes in series – bore floral, landscape, animal and maritime motifs. In 1907 the Grueby Pottery Company was set up to produce only art pottery; in 1913, however, it was dissolved. A new firm, Grueby Faience and Tile Company, was then established, which produced tiles only. It was bought in 1919 by the C Pardee Works of New Jersey, which moved the operation to its own tile factory in Perth Amboy, New Jersey.

THE J AND J G LOW ART TILES WORKS

The J and J G Low Art Tiles Works in Chelsea, founded in 1878 by a father and son both named John, produced European-style, high-gloss, solid-coloured tiles, as architectural elements and also as examples of fine art. Floral-design and animal and figural reliefs dominated its output. Among the latter were handsome, bas-relief profiles and genre scenes, known as 'plastic sketches', modelled by Arthur Osborne. These were produced as artistic entities and were sold in fancy metal frames. A 'natural process' of tile embellishment was also developed by Low, in which tiles were ingeniously adorned with impressions of actual grasses or leaves by carefully pressing the plant forms into the clay. The Low factory closed down in the early 1900s.

THE MARBLEHEAD AND PAUL REVERE POTTERIES OF MASSACHUSETTS

In the early years of the twentieth century, two Massachusetts potteries were founded as community-minded, social endeavours. The Marblehead Pottery was established to provide occupational therapy for 'nervously worn-out patients' and Arthur E Baggs was put in charge of the workshops. Marblehead's first products were unveiled to the public in around 1908 and displayed simple shades, subtle, matte glazes and stylised organic, animal and maritime motifs, sometimes painted directly onto a piece, sometimes lightly incised into it. The designs were often so conventionalised as to appear semi-abstract; straightforward geometrical patterns were used as well. 'Marblehead blue' was its best-known matte glaze, but grey, brown, red, yellow and green also appeared, sometimes three or four at a time on the earthenware bodies; tin-enamel glaze was used later on. Marblehead was always a very small enterprise, even at its peak in the 1910s, when it added maiolica to its output; operations ceased in 1937.

Boston's Paul Revere Pottery was founded in around 1906 in order to teach disadvantaged girls a craft which was both enjoyable and remunerative. Under the direction of Edith Brown and Edith Guerrier, the Saturday Evening Girls' Club flourished and soon moved to larger premises in Brighton in 1915. The earthenware products it produced were colourful, matte-glazed, useful wares – breakfast bowls, pitchers, tea tiles and nursery sets – their floral, animal and sailing-ship designs often outlined in black.

ADELAIDE ALSOP ROBINEAU

One of the luminaries of American art pottery was Adelaide Alsop Robineau, who spent most of her adult life in Syracuse, New York. She married the French-born Samuel E Robineau in 1899 and the pair, together with George Clark, bought the journal *China Decorator*, whose name they changed to *Keramic Studio*; under Adelaide's directorship the magazine

became a great success.

In 1903 Robineau herself began to experiment with various pottery techniques and glazes in the conventional *Beaux-Arts* style. She later became taken with Art Nouveau, however, and less traditional, more curvilinear and highly dramatic designs began to creep into her work. She subsequently studied with Charles F Binns at Alfred University, Alfred, New York, and was soon creating delicate, thin-walled pieces of porcelain with exquisite crystalline qualities. The Robineaus tried to

Above: A vase produced by the Paul Revere Pottery, Boston, after 1908.

Right: The 'Fox and Grapes' lidded vase by Adelaide Alsop Robineau, Syracuse, New York, c. 1920. It evokes stylised, medieval aspects, as well as the curvilinear aspects of Art Nouveau.

mass-produce her designs, but the fragile pieces did not translate well into large quantities. She turned her attention once again to individually crafted pieces and these one-off masterpieces, like her 'Scarab' vase, sold at such exclusive outlets as Tiffany & Co in New York and won awards at many major world-wide exhibitions. Her later works consisted less of highly decorative subjects and patterns and more of simpler, often oriental and Mayan motifs.

THE FULPER POTTERY

The Fulper Pottery had the longest life of all the American art potteries. Established in around 1815 (as the Samuel Hill Pottery) in Flemington, New Jersey, it first produced industrial drainpipes and tiles, later making domestic pottery. In 1909 the founder's grandson, William Hill Fulper, Jr, added art pottery, called 'vase-kraft', to its line. With its sometimes monumental, oriental-inspired shapes, the range proved extremely popular, and its ingenious lamps, whose mushroom-shaped shades bore openwork designs filled in with stained glass, were especially admired.

Although Fulper's forms were sometimes considered too clumsy, there was no disagreement on the beauty and variety of its glazes – matte, lustre, *flambé,* crystalline, spotted – which were given such fanciful names as 'Leopard Skin', 'Cucumber Green' and 'Mission Matte'.

THE SOPHIE NEWCOMB COLLEGE

In New Orleans, a pottery department was established in 1895 at the Sophie Newcomb College for Women, which developed into the source of some of America's loveliest art pottery. Its director was Elisworth Woodward, and Mary G Shearer, a china painter who had

trained with Rookwood, was instructor of design. A true Arts and Crafts spirit imbued the group, which soon evolved from a clutch of enthusiastic amateurs working with limited equipment into an organised, quasi-professional community of talented experts.

A distinctive Newcomb style resulted, whose guidelines were simplicity, sensibility and individuality. A strong sense of regionalism prevailed as well, and the flora and fauna

Below left: A tall, crystalline-glazed vase by Adelaide Alsop Robineau, Syracuse, New York, c. 1920. This vase recalls Robineau's earlier, thin-walled porcelain vessels, also covered with exquisite, crystalline glazes, resembling coloured blossoms of frost on pale, speckled grounds.

Above: A hexagonal advertising tile by Ernest A Batchelder, California.

Right: Vessels by the Newcomb College Pottery, New Orleans. At left is a covered pot, c. 1900–10; at right is a daffodil-and-leaf-decorated vase, dating from after 1910.

depicted on Newcomb's lovely, useful wares were indigenous to the area. There also grew up a characteristic Newcomb palette: soft blues, greens, pinks, yellows and creams. At first the simply shaped, low-fired, bisque vessels were underglaze-painted with stylised floral motives, their outlines often previously incised. The early, glossier wares later gave way to popular, matte-glazed wares under the influence of Paul Cox. His more muted glazes led to an overall softening of the pastel colours, as well as to a less conventional decoration.

The vases of Sadie Irvine, a gifted student who later ran the pottery department, were some of Newcomb's finest. Her most famous design, a vase featuring a dreamy landscape of moss-covered oaks, a pale-yellow moon peeping from behind the pendent moss, appeared in various permutations on many Newcomb vases.

GEORGE OHR

George Ohr, who worked at Newcomb for a short time, was noted for his strangely shaped, experimental pots. Covered with vari-coloured glazes, alone or in mottled or spotted combinations, these pieces featured such humourous elements as folded necks, crinkled ears, pinched sides or compressed rims.

Ohr worked in Biloxi, Mississippi, the coastal site of some especially desirable clays, where he perfected a method of throwing earthenware vessels whose walls were as delicately thin as those of porcelain.

ARTUS VAN BRIGGLE

As refined and sophisticated as Ohr's pots were bizarre were the vases of Artus Van Briggle's pottery in Colorado Springs. The Ohio-born Van Briggle worked for Rookwood from around 1887 and Maria Longworth Nichols was so impressed by the paintings that he exhibited at the 1893 Chicago World's Fair that she sent him to Paris to study at the Académie Julian. There he enrolled in sculpture classes, as well as painting, and his modelling in clay stood him in good stead, not only at Rookwood but also at his own small pottery.

Van Briggle's first wares at Colorado were produced in 1901, and their deeply sculptural qualities placed them firmly in the Art Nouveau vein. The matte glazes which he had been working to perfect at Rookwood were present as well, sometimes in two tones. Floral and human forms figured heavily on his wares, perhaps his best-known piece being the vase sometimes called 'Lorelei', with the long tresses and arm of a languorous woman curving round the neck of the blue-green, matte-glazed vessel, and the rest of her robed body draping around the sides. Van Briggle died in 1904, but his designs continued to be

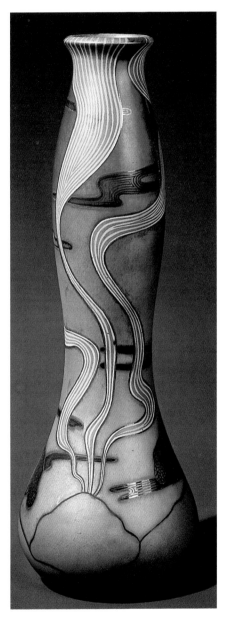

Left: A Hungarian Zsolnay vase in lustred stoneware, designed by Joszef Rippl-Ronai, c. 1890.

produced by his wife and they proved so popular that a new, enlarged facility was built in 1907.

ERNEST A BATCHELDER
A creative potter who worked on the West Coast was Ernest A Batchelder. He was a devoted admirer of the Arts and Crafts Movement, having studied at the Birmingham School of Arts and Crafts and having visited C R Ashbee's Guild of Handicraft. Batchelder was interested in oriental and Native American art, as well as in the medieval designs that inspired his British counterparts. After teaching at schools in Massachusetts, Missouri, and elsewhere, he set up his own craft school in 1909 in Pasadena, California.

Although he is best known for his striking, medievalising tile designs – cast, usually monochromatic squares featuring distinctive, conventionalised plants and animals – there were also tile series carved with landscapes that included local flora. He also produced vessels such as *jardinières* bearing bestial and avian motifs, as well as florid designs of intertwining leaves or *japoniste* branches and trees.

CONTINENTAL POTTERY
Most of the pottery being made in France, Belgium, Germany, Scandinavia and elsewhere on the European continent was in the Art Nouveau vein. More akin to Arts and Crafts was the homely, tin-glazed earthenware made the Zuidhollandsche firm at Gouda in The Netherlands, which was sold by Liberty & Co in Britain, and ceramics by Hungary's Zsolnay Ceramic Works at Pecs, renowned for its iridescent lustre glazes, especially its dark greens, blues and reds.

In Belgium, Alfred William Finch, who was of English extraction, designed earthenware

at Boch Frères' Keramis workshop. His work was sold through Henri van de Velde, the influential Belgian architect/designer who was devoted to the ideas of Ruskin and Morris. Even more directly influenced by Arts and Crafts ideals was the Wiener Werkstätte, founded in 1903 by Koloman Moser and Josef Hoffmann and modelled on C R Ashbee's Guild of Handicraft. Although the pottery produced by Wiener Keramik for the Werkstätte was clearly in the Modernist vein, with a preponderance of geometrical and other stylised motifs, the foundation on which the Viennese association was based was as idealistic as that of the Della Robbia Pottery.

FRENCH POTTERY
Of the French factory art potters, several directly influenced or even taught art potters in Britain and the United States, among them Jean-Charles Cazin, who worked in London from 1871, and Taxile Doat, the Sèvres potter who, in 1909, worked at the University City Pottery in St Louis, Missouri. Auguste Delaherche, who designed for Haviland, produced pieces which relate to many examples of American art pottery. There is a relationship, too, between Clément Massier's lustred earthenware vases and bowls, produced in Golfe-Juan – particularly in their experimental spirit – with De Morgan's pieces (a Massier employee, Jacques Sicard, was later a designer for Weller in Zanesville, Ohio).

THE INFLUENCE OF ARTS AND CRAFTS ON POTTERY
Although the Arts and Crafts Movement did not influence continental pottery in the same way as it did in Britain and America, a number of potters worked both in Britain and America, bringing the traditions of fine continental work.

Left: French stoneware vases and pears by Georges Hoentschel, Emile Grittel and Henri de Vallombreuse, c. 1900.

Below: A French stoneware vase by Albert Dammouse, c. 1900.

In America, the pottery scene was extraordinarily diverse, with small companies setting up and fading away and the larger companies producing work that attempted to jump on the Arts and Crafts bandwagon. American pottery covered the whole gamut of pieces, from domestic pottery through to high-art pottery and a renaissance in the production of decorative tiles. Both in Britain and America the Arts and Crafts Movement stimulated a huge development in art pottery which may be seen as advancing the interest in craft pottery which exists today.

Above: A French stoneware dish by Ernest Chaplet, c. 1900.